Cause and Effect

Compare and Contrast

Main Idea and Details

Steps in a Process

Literary Elements

PICTURE IT!

A Comprehension Handbook

Cause and Effect

Cause

Effect

Compare and Contrast

Main Idea and Details

Main Idea

Details

Steps in a Process

1

2

3

Literary Elements

Characters

BROTHER

MOMMY

DADDY

SISTER

Setting

Plot

Beginning

Middle

End

ISBN-13: 978-0-328-36585-2
ISBN-10:   0-328-36585-8

1 2 3 4 5 6 7 8 9 10 V063 17 16 15 14 13 12 11 10 09 08

Program Authors

Peter Afflerbach

Camille Blachowicz

Candy Dawson Boyd

Wendy Cheyney

Connie Juel

Edward Kame'enui

Donald Leu

Jeanne Paratore

Sam Sebesta

Deborah Simmons

Alfred Tatum

Sharon Vaughn

Susan Watts Taffe

Karen Kring Wixson

 PEARSON

Glenview, Illinois • Boston, Massachusetts • Mesa, Arizona
Shoreview, Minnesota • Upper Saddle River, New Jersey

Animals, Tame and Wild

THE BIG Q How are people and animals important to one another?

Animal Friends

Wild Animals

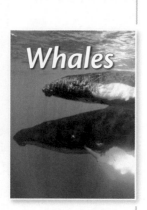

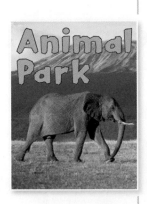

Picture It! A Comprehension Handbook PI•1- PI•5

13

Unit 1

Get Online!
PearsonSuccessNet.com

See It!
- Concept Talk Video
- Background Building Audio Slide Show
- Picture It! Animation
- e-Books

Hear It!
- Amazing Words Sing with Me
- Selection Snapshot and Response
- Paired Selection e-Text
- Grammar Jammer
- e-Books

Do it!
- Online Journal
- Story Sort
- New Literacies Activity
- Success Tracker

Animals, Tame and Wild

THE BIG ? How are people and animals important to one another?

Sam, Come Back! FICTION
Who is Sam, and where did he go?

Paired Selection
Puppy Games SING-ALONG

Pig in a Wig FANTASY
What will happen to this pig in a wig?

Paired Selection
We Are Vets SING-ALONG

The Big Blue Ox ANIMAL FANTASY
How can this big blue ox help?

Paired Selection
They Can Help PHOTO ESSAY

Whales NARRATIVE FICTION
How can people keep whales safe?

Paired Selection
Oh, Brave Bald Eagle, Soar SING-ALONG

Get the Egg! REALISTIC FICTION
Can Brad and Kim help save the red bird's egg?

Paired Selection
Help the Birds HOW-TO-ARTICLE

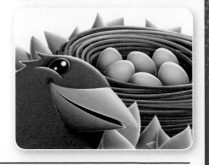

Animal Park PHOTO ESSAY
What can we see in the big park?

Paired Selection
"My Dog Rags," "Raccoon," and "The Hippo" POETRY

Let's Talk About
Animal Friends

LS1.1 Listen attentively. **LS1.4** Stay on the topic when speaking.
LS1.5 Use descriptive words when speaking about people, places, things, and events.

Words to Read

my
come
way

 R1.11 Read common, irregular sight words (e.g., *the, have, said, come, give, of*).

Read the Words

1. Sam the cat is on my lap.

2. Sam, come back!

3. He ran that way.

Genre: Fiction

Fiction stories are made-up stories. Next you will read about Sam and Jack, who are made-up characters.

Sam, Come Back!

by Susan Stevens Crummel

illustrated by Janet Stevens

Who is Sam, and
where did he go?

Sam the cat is on my lap.

Sam ran. Sam, come back!

Sam ran that way.
Nab that cat!

See Sam in the sack.

Sam ran that way.
Nab that cat!

See Sam in the pack.

Bad Sam! Sam, come back!

Jack, Jack! Sam is back.
Pat Sam on my lap.

Talk About It Did the author write a funny story? Find and read one part of the story that made you laugh.

1. Use the pictures below to retell the story. **Retell**

2. Who is Sam? Where does he run? **Character and Setting**

3. Look at pages 24 and 26. Read the words. How did you know what *nab* means? **Context Clues**

Look Back and Write Look back at pages 24–27. Sam ran away. Write about where Sam went.

Retell

R2.2 Respond to *who, what, when, where,* and *how* questions. **R2.4** Use context to resolve ambiguities about word and sentence meanings. **R2.7** Retell the central ideas of simple expository or narrative passages.

Meet the Author
Susan Stevens Crummel

Susan Stevens Crummel loves all animals. Her cat, Tweeter, likes to sit in the chair by the computer.

Ms. Crummel wrote poems and songs when she was a child. She even wrote skits for her sister Janet to act out for friends.

Read other books by Ms. Crummel.

Sing to the tune of "Frère Jacques."

Puppy Games

by Linda Lott
illustrated by Maribel Suarez

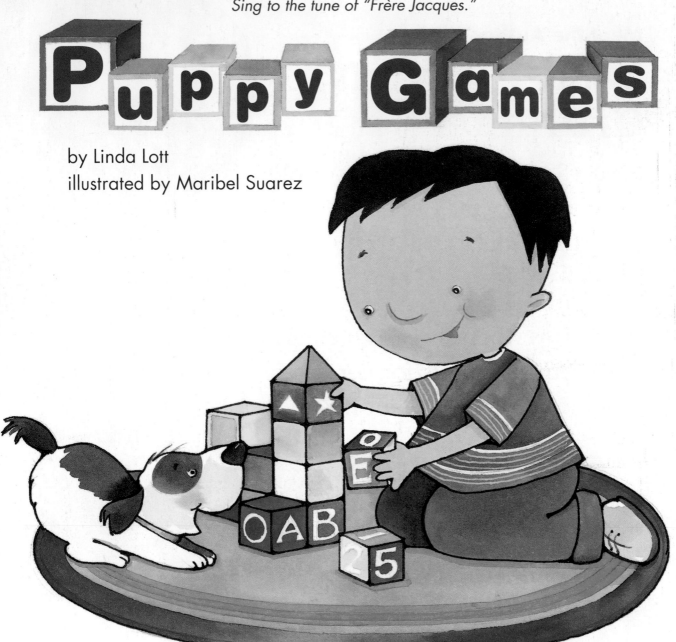

Yap! Come play now!
Yap! Come play now!
Let's have fun.
Let's have fun.

I can tug on your socks.
I'll knock over your blocks.
Then I'll nap
In your lap.

Writing Realistic Fiction

Prompt In *Sam, Come Back!* a pet has fun at play. Think about a pet you would like to have. Now write a realistic story about the pet playing.

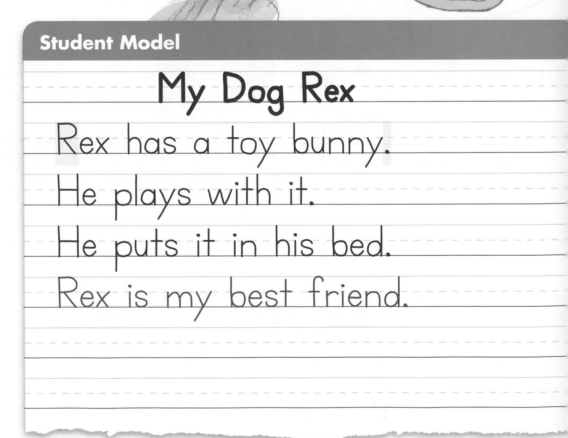

Writing Trait

Voice is the you in your sentences. It shows how you feel.

Student Model

My Dog Rex

Rex has a toy bunny.

He plays with it.

He puts it in his bed.

Rex is my best friend.

A realistic story has events that could really happen.

Sentences begin with a capital letter and end with a period.

Voice shows how the writer feels.

W1.3 Print legibly and space letters, words, and sentences appropriately.
W2.1 Write brief narratives (e.g., fictional, autobiographical) describing an experience.
LC1.5 Use a period, exclamation point, or question mark at the end of a sentence.
LC1.6 Use knowledge of the basic rules of punctuation and capitalization when writing.

Grammar Sentences

A **sentence** is a group of words that tells a complete idea. It begins with a capital letter. Many sentences end with a **period (.).**

This is a sentence   **Sam ran.**

This is not a sentence   **Al and Sam.**

Practice Look at the sentences about a pet. Name the capital letters at the beginning. Point to the periods at the end.

Let's Talk About
Animal Friends

LS1.1 Listen attentively. **LS1.4** Stay on the topic when speaking.
LS1.5 Use descriptive words when speaking about people, places, things, and events.

Words to Read

| she |
| take |
| and |
| what |

R1.11 Read common, irregular sight words (e.g., *the, have, said, come, give, of*).

Read the Words

1. She can mix.

2. She will take a sip.

3. Pig is sad, and she is sick.

4. What a ham!

Genre: Fantasy
A fantasy is a story that could not really happen. In the next story you will read about a pig that does things that a real pig can not do.

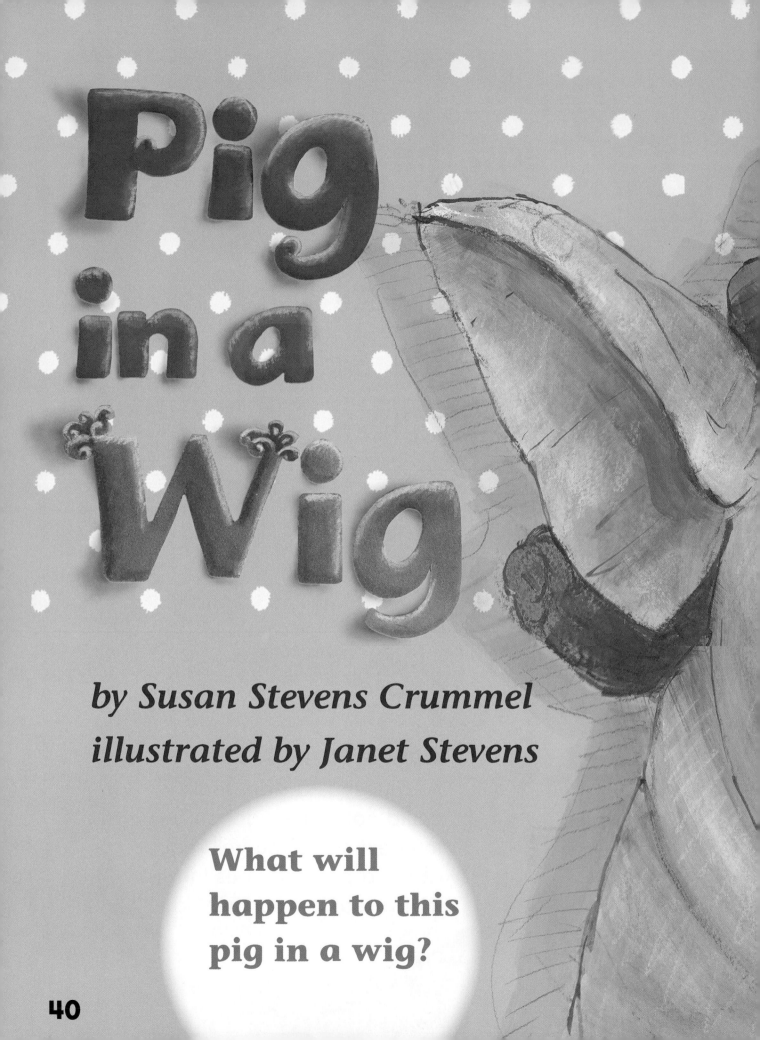

Pig in a Wig

by Susan Stevens Crummel

illustrated by Janet Stevens

What will
happen to this
pig in a wig?

41

Pig in a wig is big, you see.

Tick, tick, tick.
It is three.

Pig can mix.
Mix it up.

Pig can dip.
Dip it up.

Pig can lick.
Lick it up.

It is six. Tick, tick, tick.
Pig is sad. She is sick.

Fix that pig.
Take a sip.

Fix that pig.
Quick, quick, quick!

Max, Max! Take the sax!
Play it, Max, and play it, Pam!

Pig in a wig did a jig.
What a ham!

Talk About It The author wrote about a silly pig. Find and read one part of the story that you think is silly.

1. Use the pictures below to retell the story. Retell

2. Think about *Sam, Come Back!* and *Pig in a Wig*. How are Sam and Pig the same? How are they different? Compare and Contrast

3. Look at page 44. Read the words. How does the picture help you know what *mix* means? Monitor and Clarify

TEST PRACTICE **Look Back and Write** Look back at pages 45–47. Write what happens to this pig in a wig.

Retell

R2.2 Respond to *who, what, when, where,* and *how* questions. **R2.7** Retell the central ideas of simple expository or narrative passages. **R3.3** Recollect, talk, and write about books read during the school year.

Meet the Illustrator
Janet Stevens

Janet Stevens always wanted to draw pictures. She enjoys drawing pictures for children's books.

Ms. Stevens practices drawing all the time. "Practice helps a lot in whatever you try to do," she says. She likes to draw pigs, cats, and bears.

Read more books by Ms. Stevens.

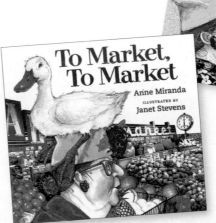

We Are Vets

by Linda Lott
illustrated by Lindsey Gardiner

Sing to the tune of "Three Blind Mice."

We are vets.
We are vets.
We help pets.
We help pets.

If you have a dog who is feeling sick,
Bring him to me, and I'll fix him quick.
His tail will wag, and he'll chase a stick.
He'll feel fine.
He'll feel fine.

Read Together

Writing Fantasy

Prompt In *Pig in a Wig*, a family helps a pet pig. Think about how people help animals. Now write a fantasy story about a person who helps an animal.

Writing Trait

Conventions are rules that make writing clear.

Each sentence has a subject.

A fantasy story has characters that do things real animals can not do.

Writer follows rules of capitalization and punctuation.

Student Model

The Pet Cow

Bob has a pet cow.

The cow likes to cook.

It makes a big mess.

Bob gives his cow a bath.

W1.3 Print legibly and space letters, words, and sentences appropriately. **W2.1** Write brief narratives (e.g., fictional, autobiographical) describing an experience. **LC1.5** Use a period, exclamation point, or question mark at the end of sentences. **LC1.7** Capitalize the first word of a sentence, names of people, and the pronoun *I*.

Writer's Checklist

✓ Does my story have characters that do things real people and animals can't do?

✓ Does each sentence begin with a capital letter and end with a period?

✓ Does each sentence have a subject?

Grammar Subjects of Sentences

A sentence has a **subject,** or naming part.
It names a person, place, animal, or thing.
The subject tells whom or what the sentence is about.

> Whom is this sentence about?
> The pig did a jig.
> **The pig** is the subject of this sentence.

Practice Look at the model.
Write the subject of each sentence.

Let's Talk About
Animal Friends

LS1.1 Listen attentively. LS1.4 Stay on the topic when speaking.
LS1.5 Use descriptive words when speaking about people, places, things, and events.

Words to Read

blue
help
little
from
use

R1.11 Read common, irregular sight words (e.g., *the, have, said, come, give, of*).

Read the Words

1. Mom and Pop have a big blue ox.

2. Ox can help a little.

3. He will get a mop from Mom.

4. He will use big pans.

Genre: Animal Fantasy

An animal fantasy is a make-believe story with animals that act like people. Next you will read about an ox that acts like a person.

The Big Blue Ox

by Susan Stevens Crummel

illustrated by Janet Stevens

How can this
big blue ox help?

63

Mom and Pop have a big blue ox.

Ox can help. He is big.
He can pick, and he can dig.

Pigs in wigs sit in mud.
Ox can help a little!

Get the mop from Mom and Pop.
Mop the pigs. Fix the wigs.

Off to town go Mom and Pop.
Ox can help! Hop on top.

Get the cans. Pack the sack.
Ox can help! Take it back.

Ox can help! Use big pans.
He is hot. Use big fans!

Mom and Pop nap on Ox.
Ox is a big, big help.

Talk About It How is Ox helpful? Find and read one part of the story that shows how helpful he is.

1. Use the pictures below to retell the story. Retell

2. Who are the characters in this story? Where does this story take place? Character and Setting

3. What pictures did you see in your mind of Ox helping? Visualize

TEST PRACTICE

Look Back and Write Look back at the story. Write some things Ox can do to help.

Retell

R2.2 Respond to *who, what, where,* and *how* questions. **R2.7** Retell the central ideas of simple expository or narrative passages. **R3.1** Identify and describe the elements of plot, setting, and character(s) in a story, as well as the story's beginning, middle, and ending.

Meet the Author and the Illustrator
Susan Stevens Crummel and Janet Stevens

Susan Crummel and Janet Stevens are sisters! They have fun working together. Ms. Crummel writes down ideas and turns them into a story. She sends the story to her sister Janet, who draws pictures to fit the story.

Read other books by Ms. Crummel and Ms. Stevens.

They Can Help

by Pat Waris

We can use help.
Can we get help?

The big dog can help.

The little dog can help.

The big dog can help.

The little dog can help.

In what ways
do they help?

Writing Animal Fantasy

Prompt In *The Big Blue Ox*, an animal helps a family. Think about an animal you know. Now write a fantasy about how that animal could help someone.

Writing Trait

Sentences tell complete ideas.

Student Model

A Good Helper
My dog helped Mom.
He cooked dinner.
Then he cleaned up.
My mom loves my dog.

Each sentence has a predicate.

A fantasy story has animals doing impossible things.

Sentences tell complete ideas.

78

W2.1 Write brief narratives (e.g., fictional, autobiographical) describing an experience. **LC1.1** Write and speak in complete, coherent sentences. **LC1.7** Capitalize the first word of a sentence, names of people, and the pronoun *I*.

Writer's Checklist

☑ Does my story have people or animals doing impossible things?

☑ Do my sentences tell complete ideas?

☑ Does each sentence have a predicate?

Grammar Predicates of Sentences

A sentence has a **predicate,** or action part. It tells what a person or thing does. Ox helps Mom and Pop.

Subject	Predicate
Ox	helps Mom and Pop.

Practice Look at the sentences about an animal that helps someone. Write the predicate in each sentence.

Let's Talk About
Wild Animals

LS1.1 Listen attentively. **LS1.4** Stay on the topic when speaking.
LS1.5 Use descriptive words when speaking about people, places, things, and events.

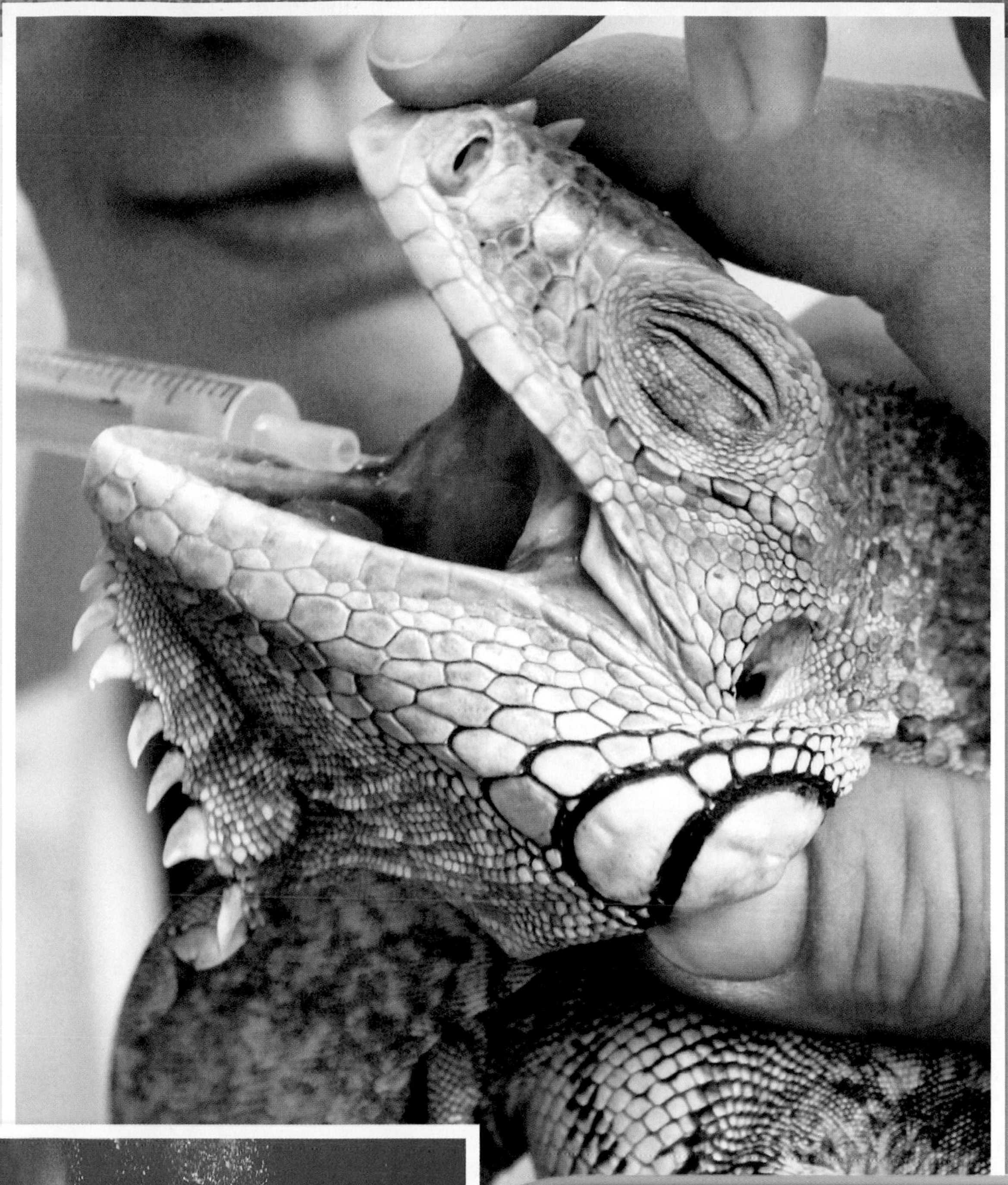

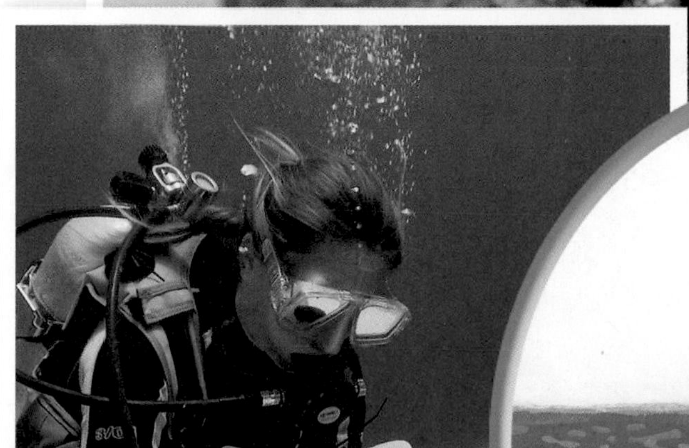

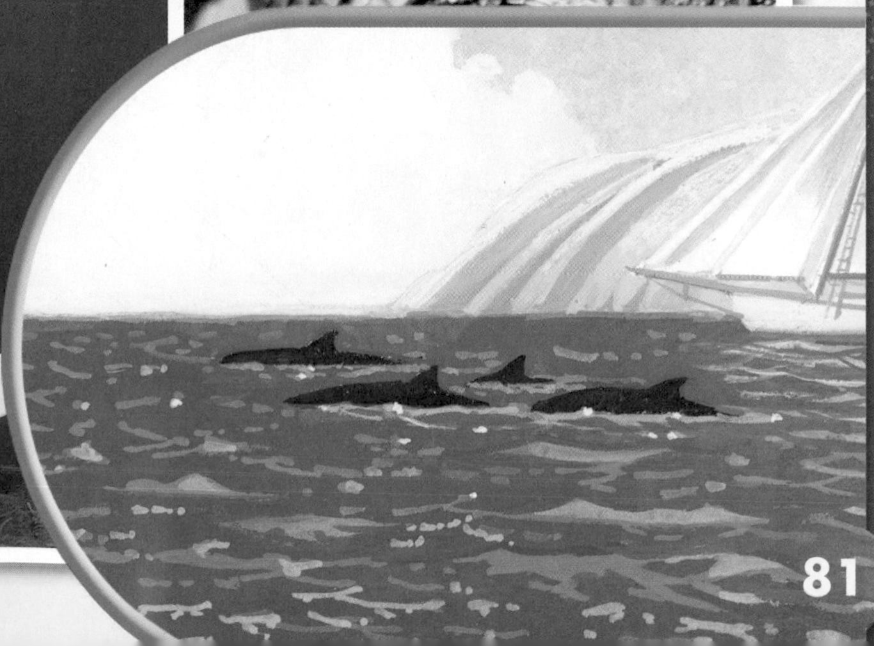

Words to Read

eat
four
five
her
this
too

  R1.11 Read common, irregular sight words (e.g., *the, have, said, come, give, of*).

Read the Words

1. Whales can eat a lot.

2. We watch four whales.

3. I can see five whales.

4. Mom hid her.

5. Let us pick up this mess too.

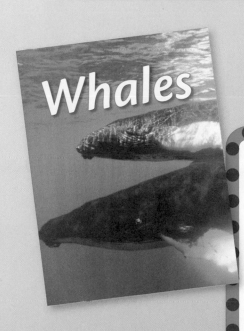

Whales

Genre: Narrative Nonfiction
Narrative nonfiction tells about real people, places, or things. Next you will read about whales and people who want to help them.

Whales

by Katacha Díaz

illustrated by Loretta Krupinski

How can people help keep whales safe?

We sit on a dock.
The whales will get here in a bit.

Quick! Here come a lot of whales!
They look like wet dots.

Whales are big animals.
They have fins on the back.
A whale eats a lot.

Mom gets us dinner.
We sit watching four big whales.

I can see five whales.
Look at that little whale.
Her big mom hid her.

Yuck! Look at this mess!
Whales can get sick.
Let us fix it up!

Kids are picking up cups.
Moms and dads are picking
up the mess too.

We did a big job.
But it is fun helping the whales.

Talk About It The author wrote *Whales* to tell us about whales. Find and read one thing you learned about whales.

1. Use the pictures below to summarize what you learned. **Summarize**

2. What is the selection mostly about? **Main Idea**

3. What questions about whales did you have as you read this selection? **Ask Questions**

TEST PRACTICE

Look Back and Write Look back at pages 91–93. Write what people can do to help whales stay safe.

Summarize

R2.7 Retell the central ideas of simple expository or narrative passages.
R3.3 Recollect, talk, and write about books read during the school year.

Meet the Author
Katacha Díaz

Katacha Díaz has wanted to be a writer ever since she was a child. In fact, she wrote her first story in a letter to her grandparents. Now Ms. Díaz gets ideas for her stories from her travels and her other interests.

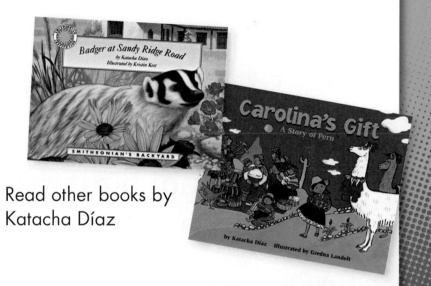

Read other books by Katacha Díaz

Oh, Brave Bald Eagle, Soar

*Sing to the tune of
"America (My Country 'Tis of Thee)."*

Oh, brave bald eagle, soar,

From every sea and shore,

Soar proud and bold.

So powerful and free,

Symbol of liberty,

National bird we see,

Behold, behold!

White feathers head and tail,
Over our land you sail,
With wings so strong.
From every mountaintop,
Your freedom will not stop,
O'er city, town, and crop,
Inspire our song!

Writing Narrative

Prompt In *Whales,* people in California help wild animals. Think about a way you helped a wild animal. Now write a personal narrative about it.

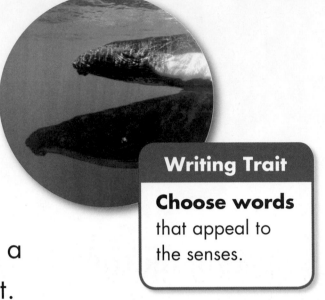

Writing Trait

Choose words that appeal to the senses.

Student Model

The Duck

I saw a duck that had a broken wing.
I wanted it to be strong and free again.
I told Mom.
She called the vet.
The vet helped the duck get better.

A personal narrative tells of an event in the author's life.

Writer chooses words that appeal to the senses.

The words are in an order that makes sense.

W1.2 Use descriptive words when writing.
W2.1 Write brief narratives (e.g., fictional, autobiographical) describing an experience.

Writer's Checklist

✓ Is my writing about an event in my own life?

✓ Do I use words that appeal to the senses?

✓ Are my sentences in an order that makes sense?

Grammar Word Order

The **order** of words in a sentence must make sense.

These words are not in the right order:
    Whales big are animals.
Now the words are in the right order:
    Whales are big animals.

Practice Check the order of the words in each sentence. Do the words make sense in this order?

Let's Talk About
Wild Animals

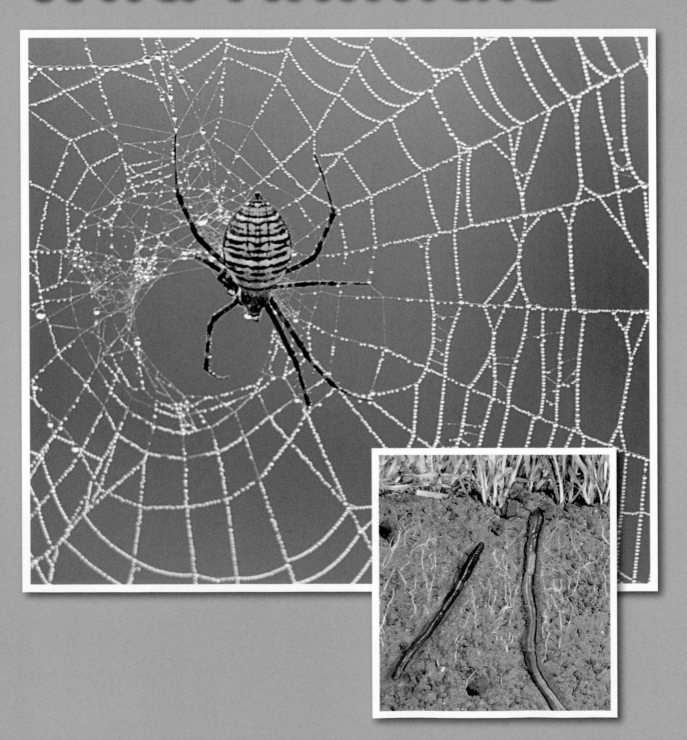

LS1.1 Listen attentively. LS1.4 Stay on the topic when speaking.
LS1.5 Use descriptive words when speaking about people, places, things, and events.

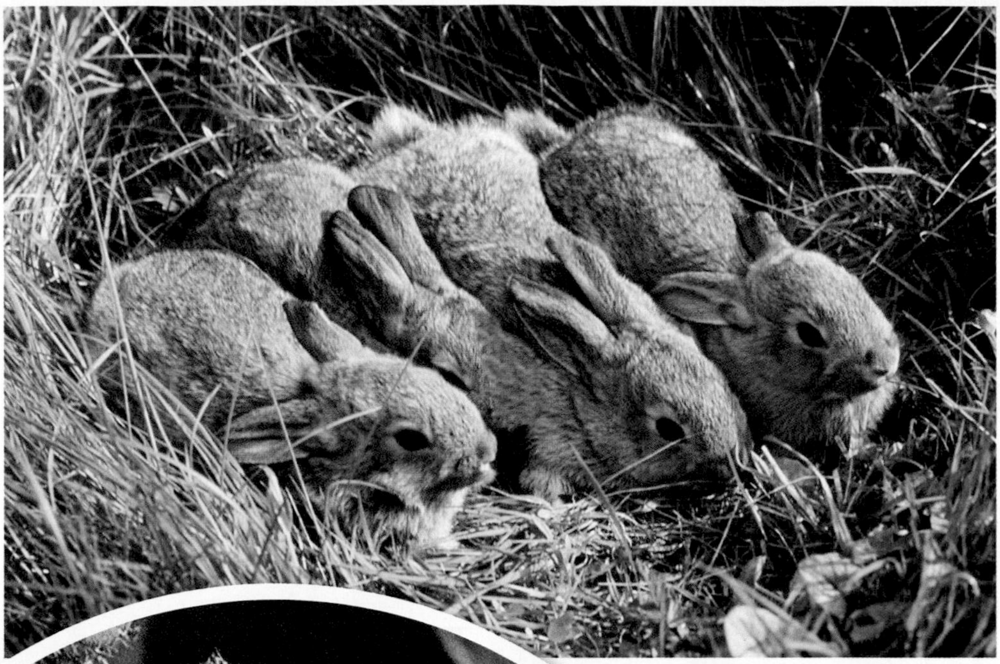

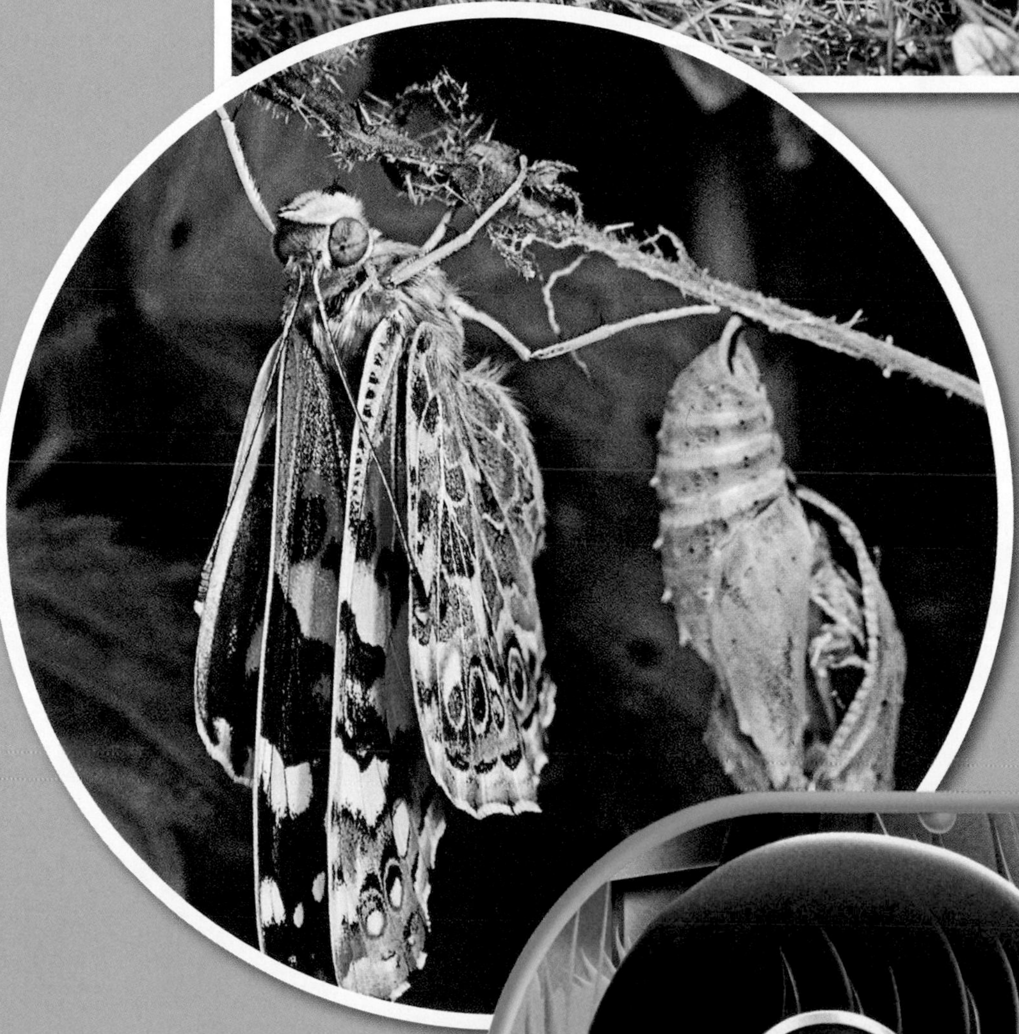

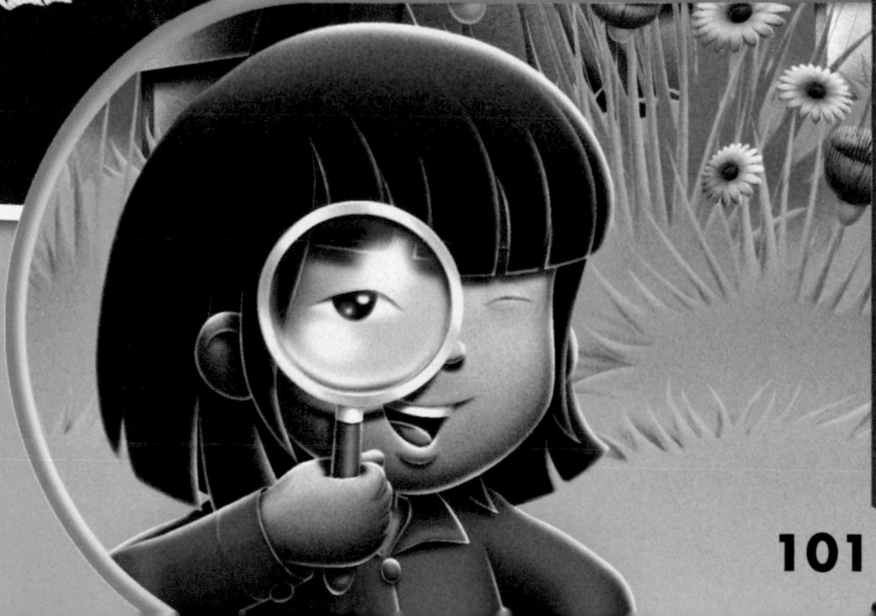

Words to Read

saw
tree
your
small

R1.11 Read common, irregular sight words (e.g., *the, have, said, come, give, of*).

Read the Words

1. Kim saw Brad.

2. Brad was at the tree.

3. I see eggs in your tree, Brad.

4. Kim and Brad saw six small eggs in the tree.

Get the Egg!

Genre: Realistic Fiction

Realistic fiction is a made-up story that could happen. In the next story you will read about a boy and a girl like you.

Get the Egg!

by Alyssa Satin Capucilli

illustrated by Bernard Adnet

Can Brad and Kim help save the red bird's egg?

Kim saw Brad at the tree.
A big red bird is in its nest, Kim.

Yes, Brad.
Six small eggs are in the nest too.

Snap! A big twig hit the nest!
Snap, snap!
The big twig hit an egg!

Stop the egg, Brad. Stop it!
Can you get the egg?

The net! Get your net, Brad.
You can help.
Get the egg in your net.

Yes! You did it, Brad.
You can help too, Kim.
Set the egg back in the nest.

Kim saw Brad at the tree.
The big red bird is back, Kim.

Yes, Brad.

The big red bird is in its nest.

Six small birds are in the nest too!

Read
Together

Talk About It This story is about a boy and a girl like you. Find and read one part of the story that you think is exciting.

1. Use the pictures below to retell the story. Retell

2. What is this story about? Main Idea

3. Look at pages 106–107. Read the words. How did you know what *nest* means? Context Clues

Look Back and Write Look back at pages 110–111. Write about how Brad and Kim save the red bird's egg.

Retell

R2.2 Respond to *who, what, when, where,* and *how* questions. R2.4 Use context to resolve ambiguities about word and sentence meanings. R2.7 Retell the central ideas of simple expository or narrative passages.

Meet the Author

Alyssa Satin Capucilli

Alyssa Satin Capucilli writes stories in a notebook she calls her "treasure keeper." Ms. Capucilli once saved a bird that had fallen from its nest. She wrote *Get the Egg!* when she remembered how proud she felt after saving the bird.

Read other books by Alyssa Satin Capucilli.

Help the Birds

Birds like to eat. You can help.

1 Get a small twig.

2 Dip it here.

3 Dip it in this.

4 Clip it to your tree.
Watch the birds come.

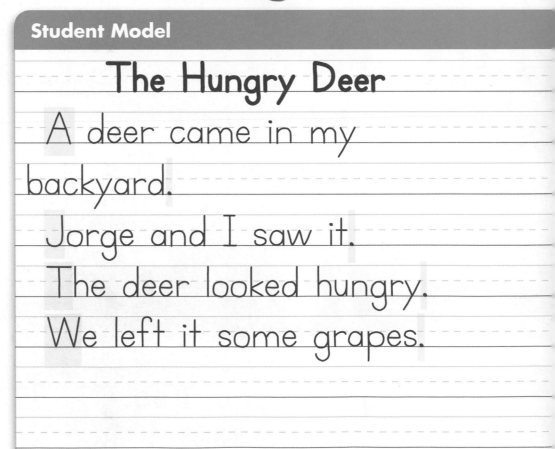

Read Together

Writing Realistic Fiction

Prompt In *Get the Egg!* two friends find a bird in their neighborhood. Think about another animal that might live in a neighborhood. Now write a realistic story about when two friends find the animal.

Writing Trait

Put your ideas in the right order.

Sentences have capital letters and periods.

A realistic story has events that can really happen.

The order of ideas in the story makes sense.

Student Model

The Hungry Deer

A deer came in my backyard.

Jorge and I saw it.

The deer looked hungry.

We left it some grapes.

Writer's Checklist

☑ Does my story have events that could really happen?

☑ Are my sentences in the right order?

☑ Does each statement begin with a capital letter and end with a period?

Grammar Statements

A **statement,** or telling sentence, tells something. It begins with a **capital letter.** It ends with a **period (.).**

Kim saw Brad at the tree**.**

Practice Look at the sentences. How do you know that they are statements?

Let's Talk About
Wild Animals

LS1.1 Listen attentively. **LS1.4** Stay on the topic when speaking.
LS1.5 Use descriptive words when speaking about people, places, things, and events.

Words to Read

home
many
them
into

R1.11 Read common, irregular sight words (e.g., *the, have, said, come, give, of*).

Read the Words

1. This is home to many big animals.

2. Will we see them?

3. We see big animals stomp into the pond.

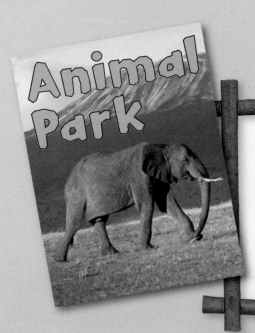

Genre: Photo Essay

A photo essay uses photos and words to explain about the real world. Next you will read about some interesting wild animals.

Africa

Animal Park

by Judy Nayer

What will we see
in the big park?

The sun is up at camp.
Camp is in a big, big park.

It is home to many animals.
Will we see them?

We go bump, bump, bump
in the truck.
A band of zebras runs past.
They blend into the grass.

Big cats rest from a hunt.
Cubs bat at bugs.

Big birds stand in the grass.
They can run fast!

Big hippos sit in mud.
The sun is hot, but the mud is not!

Are we in luck? Yes!
Big elephants stand and sip
in the pond.
They stomp into the pond and swim.

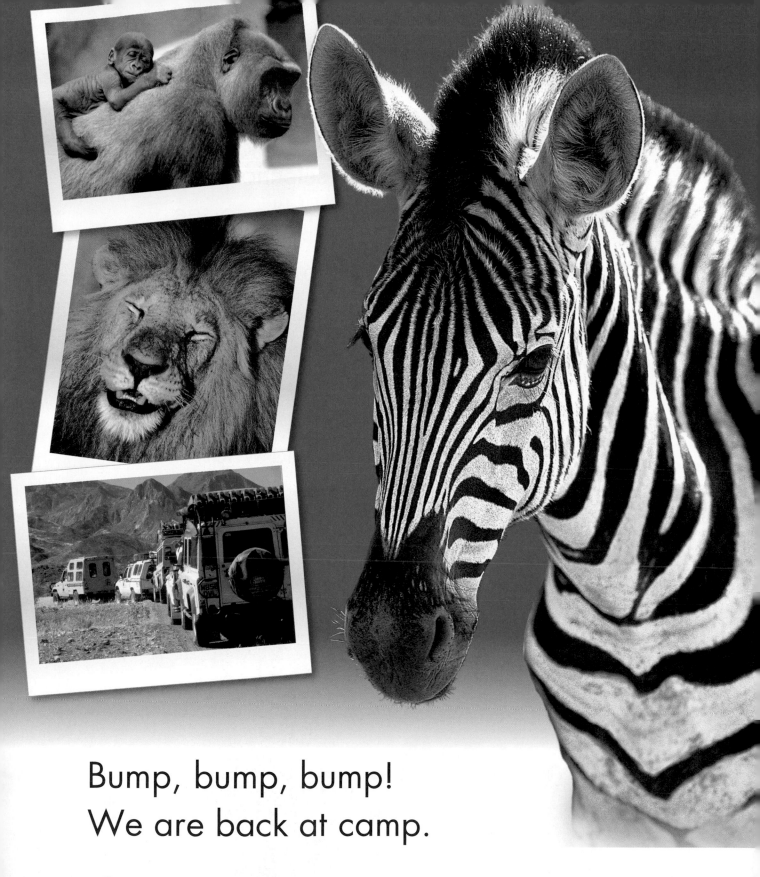

Bump, bump, bump!
We are back at camp.

This park is home to many animals.
We are glad we saw them!

Talk About It Put yourself in the animal park. Read the part of the selection that tells about the animals you would like to see.

1. Use the pictures below to summarize what you learned. Summarize

2. Why do hippos sit in the mud? Cause and Effect

3. Look at page 128. How does the picture help you understand what *blend* means? Monitor and Clarify

Look Back and Write Look back at the selection. Write about what we saw in the big park.

Summarize

R2.7 Retell the central ideas of simple expository or narrative passages.

Meet the Author
Judy Nayer

Maybe you have seen big animals in a zoo. Judy Nayer wanted to show you where some of these animals really live, in Africa. Ms. Nayer writes every day. She says, "I often work late at night, when it's very quiet."

Read more books by Judy Nayer.

Read
Together

My Dog Rags

I have a dog and his name is Rags.
He eats so much that his tummy sags.
His ears flip-flop and his tail wig-wags,
And when he walks he zig-zig-zags!

Raccoon *by Betsy Lewin*

Raccoons are not a fussy clan
when it comes time to eat.

They'll even raid a garbage can
to find a midnight treat.

136

The Hippo
by Douglas Florian

By day the hippo loves to float
On swamps and lakes, much like a boat.
At night from water it retreats,
And eats
    and eats
        and eats
           and eats.

illustrated by Patrice Aggs

Read Together

Writing Informational Article

Prompt In *Animal Park*, people visit animals in the wild. Think about what people might see wild animals doing. Now write an informational article about what people learn by watching wild animals.

Writing Trait

Sentences should **focus** on one main idea.

Student Model

Each sentence focuses on one idea.

A question has a capital letter and a question mark.

Informational articles tell about real things.

Watching Birds

I saw birds in the forest.
What did I learn?
Birds eat berries.
They live in nests.

W2.2 Write brief expository descriptions of a real object, person, place, or event, using sensory details. **LC1.2** Identify and correctly use singular and plural nouns. **LC1.5** Use a period, exclamation point, or question mark at the end of sentences. **LC1.7** Capitalize the first word of a sentence, names of people, and the pronoun *I*.

Grammar Questions

A **question** is an asking sentence. It begins with a **capital letter.**
It ends with a **question mark (?).**

Will we see the animals**?**
Are the hippos in the mud**?**

Practice Look at the model. How do you know which sentence is a question and which are statements?

Pets

cat

gerbil

kitten

guinea pig

turtle

hamster

parakeet

goldfish

puppy

dog

iguana

rabbit

Farm Animals

chick

hen

rooster

horse

goat

pig

cow

ox

calf

pony

sheep

Forest Animals

chipmunk

raccoon

turkey

skunk

opossum

bear

beaver

deer

squirrel

porcupine

Desert Animals

jack rabbit

road runner

tarantula

armadillo

iguana

camel

rattlesnake

coyote

Grassland Animals

cheetah

hyena

rhinoceros

giraffe

anteater

lion

hippopotamus

elephant

zebra

146

Water Animals

frog

lobster

octopus

clam

fish

jellyfish

shark

alligator

dolphin

manatee

whale

Cold Climate Animals

penguin

lemming

walrus

seal

polar bear

arctic fox

moose

arctic wolf

Underground Animals

mole

meercat

badger

prairie dog

earthworm

trapdoor spider

Birds

woodpecker

ostrich

goose

robin

crow

cardinal

eagle

duck

owl

hummingbird

pigeon

seagull

150

Insects and Bugs

ant

caterpillar

beetle

ladybug

cricket

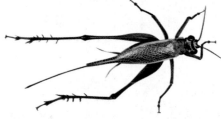

fly

lightning bug

butterfly

spider

grasshopper

bee

Sam, Come Back!

way
my
come

The Big Blue Ox

help
use
from
little
blue

Pig in a Wig

and
take
she
what

Whales

eat
her
this
too
four
five

Animal Park

home
into
many
them

Get the Egg!

saw
small
tree
your

Reading

1.0 Word Analysis, Fluency, and Systematic Vocabulary Development

Students understand the basic features of reading. They select letter patterns and know how to translate them into spoken language by using phonics, syllabication, and word parts. They apply this knowledge to achieve fluent oral and silent reading.

Concepts About Print

1.1 Match oral words to printed words.
1.2 Identify the title and author of a reading selection.
1.3 Identify letters, words, and sentences.

Phonemic Awareness

1.4 Distinguish initial, medial, and final sounds in single-syllable words.
1.5 Distinguish long- and short-vowel sounds in orally stated single-syllable words (e.g., *bit/bite*).
1.6 Create and state a series of rhyming words, including consonant blends.
1.7 Add, delete, or change target sounds to change words (e.g., change *cow* to *how; pan* to *an*).
1.8 Blend two to four phonemes into recognizable words (e.g., /c/ a/ t/ = cat; /f/ l/ a/ t/ = flat).
1.9 Segment single-syllable words into their components (e.g., /c/ a/ t/ = cat; /s/ p/ l/ a/ t/ = splat; /r/ i/ ch/ = rich).

Decoding and Word Recognition

1.10 Generate the sounds from all the letters and letter patterns, including consonant blends and long- and short-vowel patterns (i.e., phonograms), and blend those sounds into recognizable words.
1.11 Read common, irregular sight words (e.g., *the, have, said, come, give, of*).
1.12 Use knowledge of vowel digraphs and *r*- controlled letter-sound associations to read words.
1.13 Read compound words and contractions.
1.14 Read inflectional forms (e.g., *-s, -ed, -ing*) and root words (e.g., *look, looked, looking*).
1.15 Read common word families (e.g., *-ite, -ate*).
1.16 Read aloud with fluency in a manner that sounds like natural speech.

Vocabulary and Concept Development

1.17 Classify grade-appropriate categories of words (e.g., concrete collections of animals, foods, toys).

2.0 Reading Comprehension

Students read and understand grade-level-appropriate material. They draw upon a variety of comprehension strategies as needed (e.g., generating and responding to essential questions, making predictions, comparing information from several sources). The selections in *Recommended Literature, Kindergarten Through Grade Twelve* illustrate the quality and complexity of the materials to be read by students. In addition to their regular school reading, by grade four, students read one-half million words annually, including a good representation of grade-level-appropriate narrative and expository text (e.g., classic and contemporary literature, magazines, newspapers, online information). In grade one, students begin to make progress toward this goal.

Structural Features of Informational Materials

2.1 Identify text that uses sequence or other logical order.

Comprehension and Analysis of Grade-Level-Appropriate Text

2.2 Respond to *who, what, when, where,* and *how* questions.
2.3 Follow one-step written instructions.
2.4 Use context to resolve ambiguities about word and sentence meanings.
2.5 Confirm predictions about what will happen next in a text by identifying key words (i.e., signpost words).
2.6 Relate prior knowledge to textual information.
2.7 Retell the central ideas of simple expository or narrative passages.

3.0 Literary Response and Analysis

Students read and respond to a wide variety of significant works of children's literature. They distinguish between the structural features of the text and the literary terms or elements (e.g., theme, plot, setting, characters). The selections in *Recommended Literature, Kindergarten Through Grade Twelve* illustrate the quality and complexity of the materials to be read by students.

Narrative Analysis of Grade-Level-Appropriate Text

3.1 Identify and describe the elements of plot, setting, and character(s) in a story, as well as the story's beginning, middle, and ending.
3.2 Describe the roles of authors and illustrators and their contributions to print materials.
3.3 Recollect, talk, and write about books read during the school year.

Writing

1.0 Writing Strategies
Students write clear and coherent sentences and paragraphs that develop a central idea. Their writing shows they consider the audience and purpose. Students progress through the stages of the writing process (e.g., prewriting, drafting, revising, editing successive versions).

Organization and Focus
1.1 Select a focus when writing.
1.2 Use descriptive words when writing.

Penmanship
1.3 Print legibly and space letters, words, and sentences appropriately.

2.0 Writing Applications (Genres and Their Characteristics)
Students write compositions that describe and explain familiar objects, events, and experiences. Student writing demonstrates a command of standard American English and the drafting, research, and organizational strategies outlined in Writing Standard 1.0.

Using the writing strategies of grade one outlined in Writing Standard 1.0, students:
2.1 Write brief narratives (e.g., fictional, autobiographical) describing an experience.
2.2 Write brief expository descriptions of a real object, person, place, or event, using sensory details.

Written and Oral English Language Conventions

The standards for written and oral English language conventions have been placed between those for writing and for listening and speaking because these conventions are essential to both sets of skills.

1.0 Written and Oral English Language Conventions
Students write and speak with a command of standard English conventions appropriate to this grade level.

Sentence Structure
1.1 Write and speak in complete, coherent sentences.

Grammar
1.2 Identify and correctly use singular and plural nouns.
1.3 Identify and correctly use contractions (e.g., *isn't, aren't, can't, won't*) and singular possessive pronouns (e.g., *my/ mine, his/ her, hers, your/s*) in writing and speaking.

Punctuation
1.4 Distinguish between declarative, exclamatory, and interrogative sentences.
1.5 Use a period, exclamation point, or question mark at the end of sentences.
1.6 Use knowledge of the basic rules of punctuation and capitalization when writing.

Capitalization
1.7 Capitalize the first word of a sentence, names of people, and the pronoun *I*.

Spelling
1.8 Spell three- and four-letter short-vowel words and grade-level-appropriate sight words correctly.

Listening and Speaking

1.0 Listening and Speaking Strategies
Students listen critically and respond appropriately to oral communication. They speak in a manner that guides the listener to understand important ideas by using proper phrasing, pitch, and modulation.

Comprehension
1.1 Listen attentively.
1.2 Ask questions for clarification and understanding.
1.3 Give, restate, and follow simple two-step directions.

Organization and Delivery of Oral Communication
1.4 Stay on the topic when speaking.
1.5 Use descriptive words when speaking about people, places, things, and events.

2.0 Speaking Applications (Genres and Their Characteristics)
Students deliver brief recitations and oral presentations about familiar experiences or interests that are organized around a coherent thesis statement. Student speaking demonstrates a command of standard American English and the organizational and delivery strategies outlined in Listening and Speaking Standard 1.0.

Using the speaking strategies of grade one outlined in Listening and Speaking Standard 1.0, students:
2.1 Recite poems, rhymes, songs, and stories.
2.2 Retell stories using basic story grammar and relating the sequence of story events by answering *who, what, when, where, why,* and *how* questions.
2.3 Relate an important life event or personal experience in a simple sequence.
2.4 Provide descriptions with careful attention to sensory detail.

Acknowledgments

Text

Page 136: "Raccoon" from *Animal Snackers* by Betsy Lewin. © 1980, 2004 by Betsy Lewin. Reprinted by permission of Henry Holt and Company, LLC.

Page 136: Excerpt from "The Hippo" in *Mammalabilia,* text copyright © 2000 by Douglas Florian, reprinted by permission of Harcourt, Inc. This material may not be reproduced in any form or by any means without the prior written permission of the publisher.

Illustrations

Cover: Daniel Moreton; PI2-P17 Mary Anne Lloyd; 18-29, 38-50, 62-71 Janet Stevens; 32-33 Maribel Suarez; 54-55 Lindsey Gardiner; 86-92 Loretta Krupinski; 96 Donald Wu; 104-113 Bernard Adnet; 136-137 Patrice Aggs

Photographs

Every effort has been made to secure permission and provide appropriate credit for photographic material. The publisher deeply regrets any omission and pledges to correct errors called to its attention in subsequent editions.

Unless otherwise acknowledged, all photographs are the property of Scott Foresman, a division of Pearson Education.

Photo locators denoted as follows: Top (T), Center (C), Bottom (B), Left (L), Right (R), Background (Bkgd).

16 ©Frank Siteman/Stock Boston

17 (T) ©Myrleen Ferguson Cate/PhotoEdit, (C) ©Royalty-Free/Corbis; 36 ©LWA- JDC/Corbis

37 (TL) ©Kaz Chiba/Getty Images, (TR) ©The York Dispatch/Jason Plotkin/AP/Wide World Photos, (C) Tracy Morgan/©DK Images

58 (B) ©Steve Thornton/Corbis, (T) ©Royalty-Free/Corbis

59 (C) ©Alan Oddie/PhotoEdit, (T) ©Royalty-Free/Corbis

74 Getty Images

75 ©Mark Richards/PhotoEdit

76 ©Peter Olive/Photofusion Picture Library/Alamy Images

77 (TL) ©Bryan and Sherry Alexander Photography, (TR) ©A. Ramey/PhotoEdit, (C) ©Dallas and John Heaton/Corbis

80 ©Mast Irham/epa/Corbis

81 (T) ©Waltraud Grubitzsch/dpa/Corbis, (BL) ©Nicole Duplaix/National Geographic Image Collection; 84 ©Jeff Hunter/Getty Images

88 (CL) ©Gerard Lacz/Animals Animals/Earth Scenes, (CR) ©Brandon Cole Marine Photography/Alamy Images, (BL) ©DLILLC/Corbis, (BR) ©James Watt/Animals Animals/Earth Scenes

98 ©Jeff Hunter/Getty Images

100 (B) ©Jean Paul Ferrero/Ardea, (T) ©Niall Benvie/Corbis

101 (T) ©Dennis Avon/Ardea, (C) ©John Mason (JLMO)/Ardea; 120 ©Paul Souders/Corbis

121 (TR) ©Ron Sachs/Sygma/Corbis, (C) ©David Muench/Corbis, (TL) ©Michael & Patricia Fogden/Corbis, (BR) ©Peter Johnson/Corbis

124 (TL) Getty Images, (Bkgd) ©Tim Davis/Corbis

126 (Bkgd) ©Photo Researchers, Inc., (BR) ©Craig Lovell/Corbis; **127** (L) ©Staffan Widstrand/Corbis, (TR, BR) Digital Stock, (CR) Digital Vision

128 (Bkgd) ©Tom Nebbia/Corbis, (TC) Jupiter Images

129 (TC) ©Tom Brakefield/Corbis, (CC) ©Art Wolfe Inc.

130 (TC) ©Beverly Joubert/NGS Image Collection, (BC) ©Peter Johnson/Corbis

132 ©Theo Allofs/Getty Images

133 (TL) Brand X Pictures, (CL) ©Norbert Rosing/NGS Image Collection, (BL) ©David Young-Wolff/Alamy Images, (Bkgd) Digital Vision

135 Courtesy Judy Nayer

140 (CL) Karl Shone/©DK Images, (TR) Jane Burton/©DK Images, (CC) ©Richard Kolar/Animals Animals/Earth Scenes, (TL) Marc Henrie/©DK Images, (B) Getty Images, (CR, BR) Paul Bricknell/©DK Images

141 (T) ©DK Images, (BR, BL) Ingram Publishing

142 (BL, CR) Dave King/©DK Images, (BR) ©DK Images, (TR) Gordon Clayton/©DK Images, (TC) Mike Dunning/©DK Images, (TL) Jane Burton/©DK Images

143 (BL) Bob Langrish/©DK Images, (T, CR, BR) Gordon Clayton/©DK Images, (CL) ©Ike Geib/Grant Heilman Photography

144 (TCL) ©Dr. Harvey Barnett/Peter Arnold, Inc., (TL) ©Gary W. Carter/Corbis, (BL) Jane Burton/©DK Images, (TC) ©W. Perry Conway/Corbis, (BBC) ©S. J. Krasemann/Peter Arnold, Inc., (CR) ©Dave King/©DK Images, (BR) ©G. K. & Vikki Hart/Getty Images, (TR) Getty Images, (BCL) Jupiter Images, (CC) ©Corbis Premium RF/Alamy

145 (BL) Philip Dowell/©DK Images, (CL) Getty Images, (TR) ©DK Images, (BCR) Dave King/©DK Images, (TL) ©Daniel Sweeney (escapeimages)/Alamy, (TC) ©Steve Hamblin/Alamy, (TCR) ©VStock/Index Open, (BR) ©imagebroker/Alamy

146 (CL) ©Jim Zuckerman/Corbis, (BR) ©DK Images, (BCC) Dave King/©DK Images, (CR) ©David Madison/Bruce Coleman Inc., (BL) Philip Dowell/©DK Images, (TCC) ©Tony Phelps/Alamy, (TR) ©Juniors Bildarchiv/Alamy, (TCC) ©Ablestock/Alamy, (TL) ©Nature Picture Library/Alamy

147 (TC) Colin Keates/©DK Images, (BL) ©Frank Staub/Index Stock Imagery, (BCC) ©Jim Stamates/Getty Images, (TR) Frank Greenaway/©DK Images, (TCC, TCR) Getty Images, (TL) ©DK Images, (BCL) ©Lionel Isy-Schwart/Getty Images, (BCR) Digital Stock, (BR) ©Brandon D. Cole/Corbis, (TCL) ©Kevin Moore/Alamy

148 (TL) ©Galen Rowell/Corbis, (CR) ©Ralph Lee Hopkins/Wilderland Images, (CC) ©Nigel McCall/Alamy, (TC, TCL) Getty Images, (BR) ©Corbis Premium RF/Alamy, (BCL) ©David Hosking/Alamy Images

149 (TL, C) Index Open, (BR) ©Stefan Sollfors/Alamy, (TR) ©Emile Wessels/Alamy, (CL) ©Corbis Premium RF/Alamy, (BL) ©Hans Christoph Kappel/Nature Picture Library

150 (TL) ©Roy Rainford/Robert Harding World Imagery, (BL) ©Ray Coleman/Photo Researchers, Inc., (TR) ©Tom McHugh/Photo Researchers, Inc., (BCL) ©Jeff Lepore/Photo Researchers, Inc., (BCR) ©Bill Dyer/Photo Researchers, Inc., (BCC, BCR) Cyril Laubscher/©DK Images, (BC) ©John Edwards/Getty Images, (BR) ©Dinodia/Omni-Photo Communications, Inc., (TCL) ©Arthur Morris/Corbis, (TCC) ©Darrell Gulin/Corbis, (TCC) Digital Vision

151 (TCL) Neil Fletcher/©DK Images, (TCC) ©Simon D. Pollard/Photo Researchers, Inc., (BC, BR) Frank Greenaway/©DK Images, (TL) Jupiter Images, (TC) ©Cyndy Black/Robert Harding World Imagery, (CR) ©Rudi Von Briel/PhotoEdit, (BCL) ©DK Images, (TR) Colin Keates/©DK Images, (BCC) Robert & Linda Mitchell, (BL) Getty Images

Reading
STREET

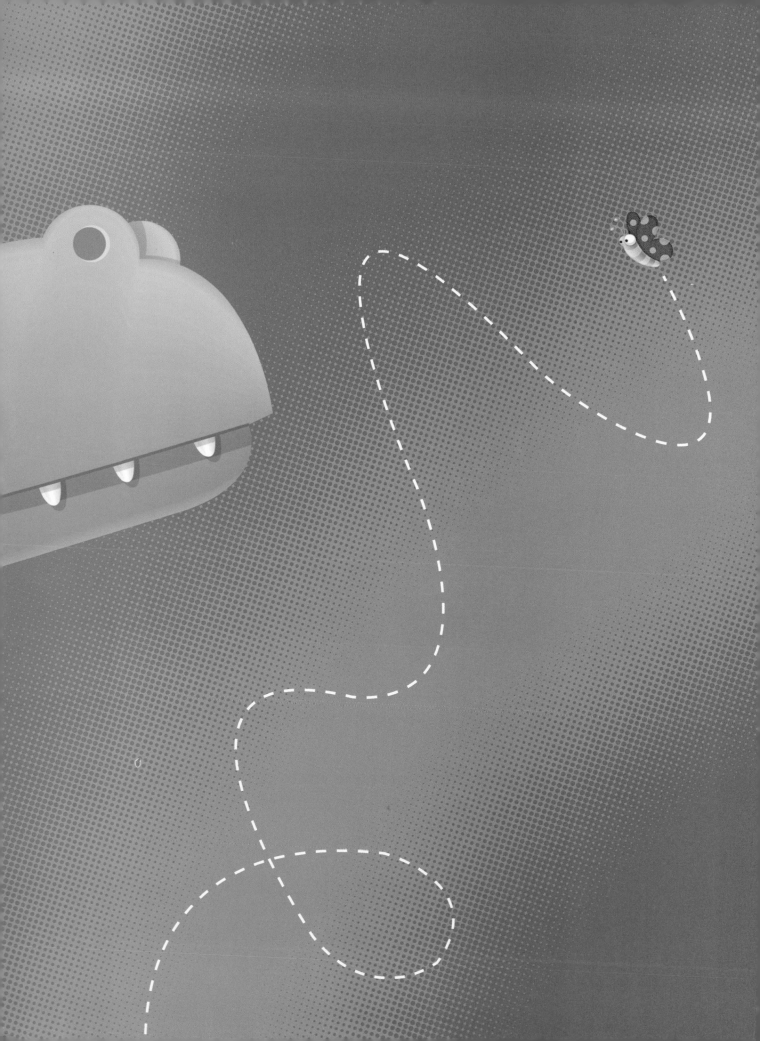